EAU CLAIRE DISTRICT LIBRARY
6528 East Main Street
P.O. Box 328
EAU CLAIRE, MI 49111

388

Fec

EAU CLAIRE DISTRICT LIBRARY
6528 East Main Street
P.O. Box 328
EAU CLAIRE, MI 49111

Ladders

On the Move

World Book

in association with
WCN

EAU CLAIRE DISTRICT LIBRARY

T 137504

World Book, Inc.
233 N. Michigan Ave.
Chicago, IL 60601
in association with Two-Can Publishing.

For information about other World Book publications, visit our
Web site http://www.worldbook.com or call 1-800-WORLDBK
(967-5325). For information about sales to schools and libraries,
call 1-800-975-3250 (United States); 1-800-837-5365 (Canada).

Written and edited by: Sarah Fecher and Deborah Kespert
Story by: Belinda Webster
Consultants: Dr. Iram Siraj-Blatchford, Institute of Education, London; David Glover
Art director: Belinda Webster
Design: Amanda McCourt
Main illustrations: Gaëtan Evrard
Computer illustrations: Jon Stuart
U.S. Editor: Sharon Nowakowski, World Book Publishing

2006 Printing
© Two-Can Publishing, 1998

All rights reserved. No part of this publication may be reproduced,
stored in a retrieval system, or transmitted in any form or by any
means electronic, mechanical, photocopying, recording, or otherwise,
without prior written permission of the publisher.

"Two-Can" is a trademark of Two-Can Publishing.

Library of Congress Cataloging-in-Publication Data
Fecher, Sarah.
    On the move / [written and edited by Sarah Fecher and Deborah Kespert; story by Belinda Webster; main
illustrations, Gaëtan Evrard; computer illustrations, Jon Stuart].
        p. cm. — (Ladders)
    Includes index.
    Summary: Introduces various modes of transportation, including bicycles, buses, and helicopters. Includes
related story and activities.
        ISBN 0-7166-7711-3 (hc) — ISBN 0-7166-7712-1 (sc)
        1. Transportation—Juvenile literature. [1. Transportation.] I. Kespert, Deborah. II. Webster, Belinda. III. Evrard,
Gaëtan, ill. IV. Stuart, Jon, ill. V. Title. VI. Series.
TA1149.F43   1998
388—dc21 ·   97-32800

Photographic credits: p4: Allsport UK Ltd; p5: Telegraph Colour Library; p7: Quadrant Picture Library;
p9 top: Robert Harding Picture Library; bottom: Britstock- IFA; p10: James Davis Travel Photography;
p12: Pictor International; p13: Pictor International; p17: Britstock- IFA; p18: Zefa; p19: Tony Stone Images;
p21: Tony Stone Images; p22: Tony Stone Images.

Printed in China

7 8 9 10 09 08 07 06

What's inside?

This book tells you about lots of exciting ways to travel. You can find out how cars and trains speed over land, how boats float across water, how airplanes soar through the sky, and more!

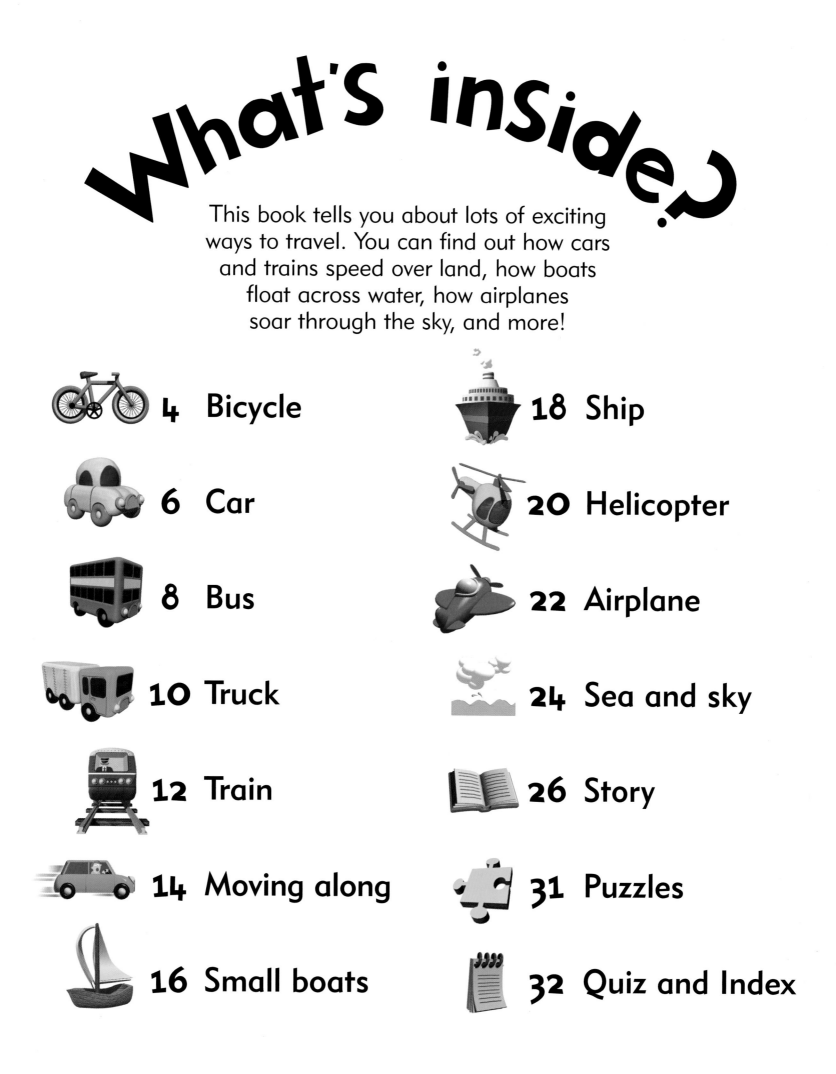

 # Bicycle

Bicycles are lots of fun. You can cycle to the park with your friends or to the stores. It is easy to learn how to ride a bicycle. You may wobble at first, but soon you will be pedaling like a pro!

A light-weight racing bicycle speeds along a track. The rider dips his body and head, letting the air rush past.

Always wear a hard **helmet** to protect your head.

To ride a bicycle, you sit on the seat and push the **pedals** with your feet.

A **mudguard** helps keep you dry when you splash through a puddle.

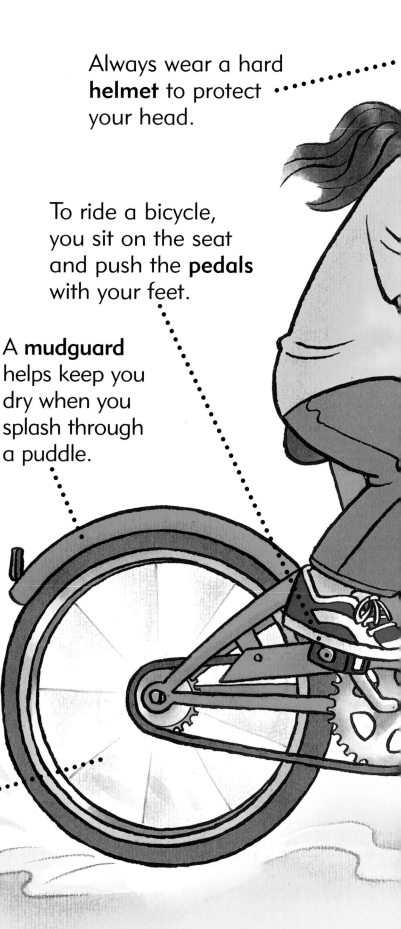

Two **wheels** spin around and move the bicycle forward.

Holding the **handlebars** keeps you steady and lets you steer.

You can ring your **bell** to warn people that you are coming.

A rickshaw has three wheels and a comfortable back seat. You sit inside and a driver cycles you across town.

When you squeeze the brake on the handlebar, a **brake pad** rubs against the wheel to slow you down.

It's a fact!

A unicycle has one wheel and no handlebars. It takes time and a lot of balance to learn how to ride one!

Car

All over the world, people travel by car. Cars can hold the whole family, and they can go wherever there are roads. Cars are quick too, but watch out—there may be a traffic jam ahead!

It's a fact!

The world's longest car has 26 wheels. There is even a swimming pool onboard so that you can take a quick dip!

Turning the **steering wheel** makes the car turn left or right.

An **engine** uses fuel to make the car move.

At night, the car's bright **lights** light up the road.

Thick **tires** grip the road, even in wet weather.

You can pile extra luggage onto the **roof rack**.

A race car zooms around a track as fast as it can. Before the race, a team of helpers check that the car works properly.

Everybody helps load luggage into the **trunk** for the journey.

Wearing a **seat belt** helps keep you safe.

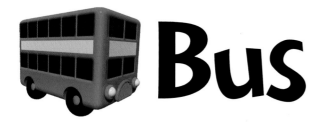 # Bus

Buses pick people up and drop them off at bus stops all over town. There is room for lots of people inside. As you ride the bus, you can look out the windows and watch for your stop.

You wait for a bus at a **bus stop**.

You read the **schedule** to find out when your bus will arrive.

Inside, the **passengers** sit on seats.

The **doors** open to let everybody climb on board.

You need to pay **money** for your ride.

A **sign** tells you where the bus is going.

TOWN SQUARE

The **driver** can see the road clearly through the big front windows.

A minibus is full inside, so people tie their packages to the roof!

A double-decker bus chugs through the city. You can sit down below or climb upstairs to the seats on top.

Truck

Trucks come in different shapes and sizes. They rumble down roads, moving all kinds of heavy loads from place to place. Trucks can deliver ice-cold drinks and fresh bread to a shop, or take your furniture to a new home.

This long truck carries oil in two huge, shiny containers. The driver travels for days to deliver the load.

There is plenty of space inside the **trailer** to pile up your belongings.

Movers walk down a **ramp** to reach the ground.

Packing things in strong **boxes** keeps them safe.

The front part of the truck is called the **cab**. This is where the driver and a helper sit.

It's a fact!

The world's highest truck has wheels as tall as two people. You reach the cab by climbing up a ladder!

A large **mirror** makes it easy for the driver to see the road behind.

Movers climb up a **step** to get into the cab.

A new sofa is a heavy **load**. It is hard work carrying it to the house!

Train

All day long, trains hurry from town to town. They stop at stations along the way to let people step on and off. A train moves quickly, racing past fields, over bridges, and through deep, dark tunnels.

This is the TGV, the world's fastest train. It rushes people to distant cities twice as fast as a car on a highway.

Passengers sit in **coaches** that are hooked together in a long line.

Zooming through a **tunnel** in a mountain is faster than trudging up and over a mountain.

A train rolls along two shiny rails called **railroad tracks**.

The engineer moves **levers** to make the train speed up or slow down.

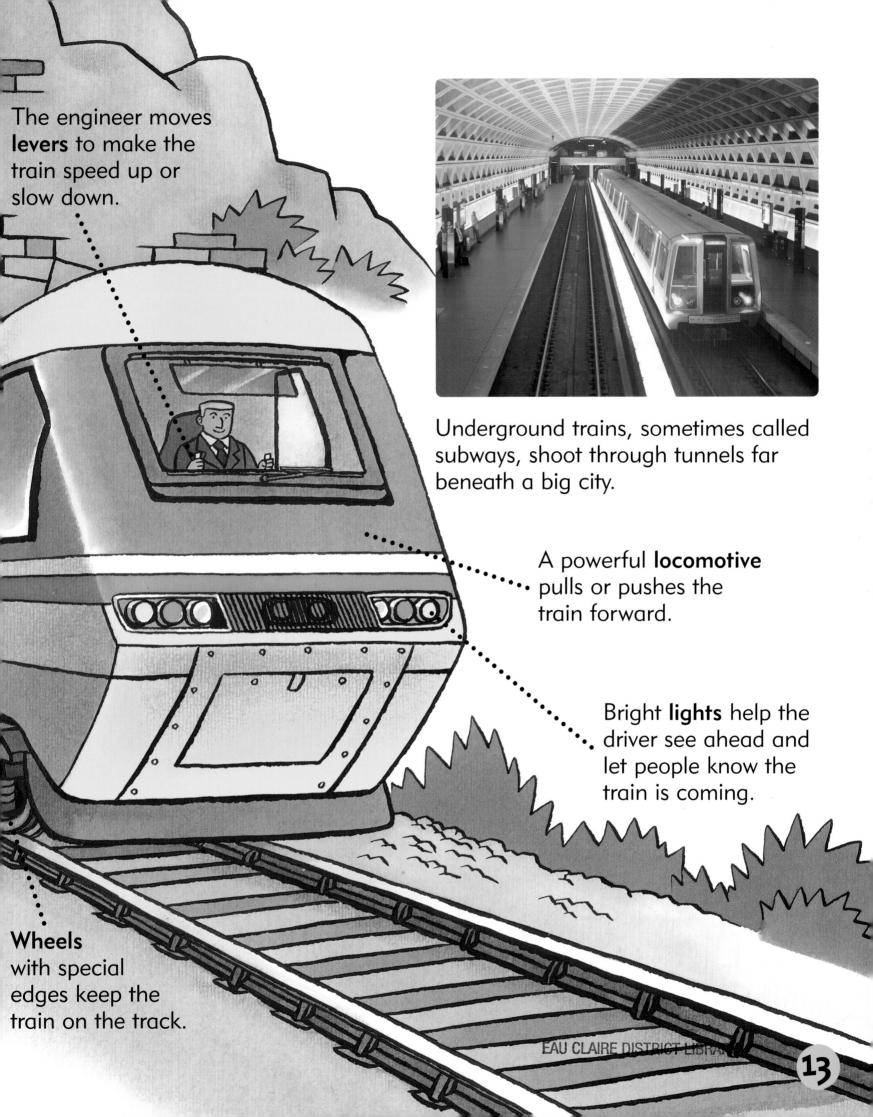

Underground trains, sometimes called subways, shoot through tunnels far beneath a big city.

A powerful **locomotive** pulls or pushes the train forward.

Bright **lights** help the driver see ahead and let people know the train is coming.

Wheels with special edges keep the train on the track.

EAU CLAIRE DISTRICT LIBRARY

Moving along

Today the town is packed with lots of people going to different places. They are in cars, trucks, and buses, and on bikes!

How many people are riding bicycles?

14

Where is the bus stop?

Which car looks like it has engine trouble?

Words you know

Here are words that you read earlier in this book. Say them out loud, then try to find the things in the picture.

passengers **trailer** **wheels**
coaches **helmet** **engine**

What is the fast train zooming into?

Small boats

Floating on the water in a small boat is great fun. You can sit in a sailboat, like the one in the big picture, and let the wind blow you gently along. A sailboat often tips and rolls in the waves, so remember to hold on tight!

A **life jacket** helps keep you safe if you fall into the water.

The wind blows against a large **sail** and pushes the boat forward.

To go faster, you pull on a thick **rope**.

You move the **rudder** to make the sailboat turn.

A tall, strong **mast** holds up the sail.

Paddling a kayak can be hard work! You push the long paddle through the water to move the boat along.

The **hold** is a good place to store a picnic!

The **hull** floats in the water. There is room for a few people to sit inside.

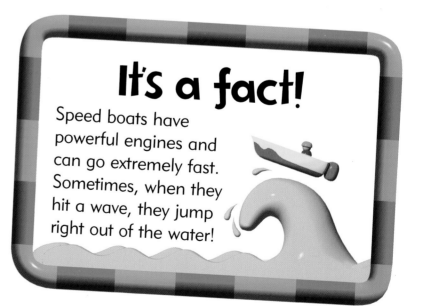

It's a fact!

Speed boats have powerful engines and can go extremely fast. Sometimes, when they hit a wave, they jump right out of the water!

Ship

Ships are giant boats. Many ships cross the big oceans to places on the other side of the world. Ferries, like the one in the big picture, carry people on short journeys. One end opens up to let people drive on board.

It's a fact!

Oil tankers are the world's longest ships. You need a bicycle to travel from one end to the other!

A cruise ship slowly glides through the warm blue sea. It is taking hundreds of people on a faraway vacation.

People wait at the **dock** before driving onto the ferry.

People park their cars on the **car deck**.

Smoke puffs out of the **smokestack**.

The **captain** is in charge of the ferry and steers it out of the dock.

On the **top deck**, you can sit on seats and chat.

From inside, you can look out of large **portholes**.

This cargo ship carries heavy boxes, packed with goods. Huge cranes lift the boxes onto the ship.

Helicopter

Have you ever seen a helicopter whirling in the sky? It can fly straight up and down and even hover (stay in one place). Helicopters have many jobs. Some help people watch the traffic below, others take people sightseeing!

A **pilot** sits at the front and flies the helicopter.

The pilot moves a **joy stick** to make the helicopter go up and down or stay still.

A **headset** lets the pilot talk to people on the ground.

The helicopter lands gently on its two strong **skids**.

It's a fact!

A helicopter can land in a small space. It can even squeeze onto the top of a high building in a busy city.

Flat **blades** whirr around and lift the helicopter into the air.

This helicopter carries people to work at sea and takes them home many months later. It lands on a special platform called a helipad.

A long **tail** with spinning blades at the end keeps the helicopter steady.

Passengers sit in the bubble-shaped **cabin** and look at the amazing view!

Airplane

Airplanes take off and land at airports. They fly high above the clouds, carrying people to different cities and countries. In an airplane, you can fly across the world in a day!

These decorated airplanes take part in air shows. They fly side by side, twisting and turning in the sky.

A baggage truck carries piles of suitcases to the **hold**.

Huge **wings** help the airplane soar through the air.

An airplane speeds along the runway and **takes off**.

It's a fact!

One unusual plane can fly in space! It is called the space shuttle and can loop around Earth in just over one hour.

A pilot sits high up in the **cockpit** behind the controls.

Passengers climb up the steps and a **flight attendant** welcomes them on board.

An airplane has strong **wheels** to help it land smoothly on the runway.

Sea and sky

The sea and sky are full of people moving about! Some are having fun and others are going on a journey.

Words you know

Here are some words that you learned earlier. Say them out loud, then try to find the things in the picture.

rudder	wings	sail
portholes	car deck	cabin

24

25

Where is the helicopter pilot?

The curious bus driver

"I like driving my bus," thought the bus driver. "But I drive at the same time every day, down the same streets, and wait at the same bus stops." As he dropped off his last passenger he asked himself, "I wonder what it would be like to do something different for a change?"

In the middle of the night, the curious bus driver woke up with a brilliant idea. "I know what I'm going to do," he whispered to his cat. "I'll put an advertisement in the newspaper and see if anyone replies."

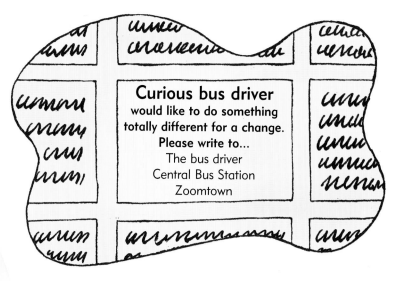

Curious bus driver would like to do something totally different for a change. Please write to... The bus driver Central Bus Station Zoomtown

The next day, two enormous sacks of letters arrived. They were all from people inviting him to do something totally different for a change.

The bus driver sat down and sorted them into "yes" and "no" piles. He immediately wrote back to thank the people in the "no" pile for their kind invitations. Then, in the afternoon, he telephoned the people in the "yes" pile to make plans for the following week.

This is what he wrote on his calendar so he wouldn't forget when he was going to meet everybody.

Monday   airplane pilot
Tuesday   subway engineer
Wednesday   race car driver
Thursday   ferry boat captain
Friday   day off

"I'm going to fly with a pilot today," chuckled the bus driver, when he woke up on Monday morning. He stretched his arms out like wings and leaped out of bed.

It was not a good day to fly. The sky was dark and scary and the rain was as heavy as nails.

When he arrived at the airport, he looked around for the pilot. She was easy to spot in her smart uniform with sparkly gold stripes.

"Pleased to meet you," she said, shaking his hand. "I'm afraid I can't fly my plane in the middle of a severe storm. Let's have a cup of tea while we wait until the weather brightens up."

The bus driver followed the pilot into the cockpit. He sat down in a little seat surrounded by colored lights and switches. They drank lots of cups of tea, and the pilot taught him some complicated card tricks. The pilot told him exciting stories about flying her plane, but the rain kept them on the ground.

"Flying a plane must be hard work," thought the bus driver as he looked out at the rain flooding the runway. "I'm glad I don't have to do it, especially in bad weather like this!"

When the day was finally over, the bus driver thanked the pilot for the interesting conversation and for the cups of tea.

On Tuesday morning, the storm had disappeared and it was a perfect, sunny day.

"I'm going to meet a subway engineer today," laughed the bus driver as he crawled under his bed to find his missing sock.

He arrived at the subway station on time and rode an escalator down to the train waiting at the platform.

"Hop in," called the engineer. "I've been expecting you."

They spent the whole day whizzing through dark, windy tunnels, and stopping at platforms. The subway engineer was very generous and shared his last piece of strawberry bubble gum.

The round walls of the dark, twisty tunnels flashed by as the train sped along underground.

"This sure is a fast way to travel," thought the bus driver. "But I really miss chatting with my passengers and looking at the beautiful sky."

When the day was over, the bus driver thanked the engineer for sharing his strawberry bubble gum and for showing him around under the city.

On Wednesday morning, the bus driver woke up feeling excited.

"I'm going to meet a race car driver today," he shouted as he ran to the bathroom.

When he arrived at the race track there was a brand new, shiny, red race car to meet him.

"Squeeze in," said the driver from under his helmet. The bus driver climbed into the car, put on a helmet, and fastened his seat belt as tight as he could.

"Go as fast as you can!" he yelled.

The race car zoomed off around and around the race track, cutting corners and flying over bumps. The engine was so noisy that they could only hear each other talking if they shouted. The race

car driver told lots of funny jokes at the top of his voice. The bus driver laughed and laughed, but soon he felt dizzy from going around too many times and from laughing so much.

"Imagine if I went this fast in my bus," giggled the bus driver. "All my passengers' packages would fly everywhere and I'd never hear them ring the bell to let them off."

When the day was over, the bus driver thanked the race car driver for going really fast in his shiny red race car.

On Thursday morning, the bus driver woke up really early.

"I'm going to meet the captain of a ferry," he sang at the top of his voice as he stood under the shower.

When he arrived at the harbor, the ferry was docked and lots of cars and trucks were lining up to drive on board. He could see someone waving at him from the top deck.

"Climb aboard!" yelled the captain.

The bus driver went up to a room at the top of the ferry with huge windows and a beautiful view of the sea. He stood next to the captain and helped her steer the ferry out of the harbor.

The captain showed the bus driver how to steer the boat. She also taught him how to whistle to the sea gulls.

The day was crisp and windy, and out at sea, the waves were choppy. The bus driver started to feel a little seasick.

"I think I'm better off on flat, dry land," he said. "It's hard to walk around on this bouncy boat."

"It does take getting used to," the captain replied, and she whistled some more to cheer up the bus driver.

When the day was over, the bus driver thanked the captain for letting him steer the ship.

"It's my day off today," yawned the bus driver, when he woke up Friday morning. "What an exciting week I've had. I talked to a pilot and saw the plane's big engines and twinkling lights. I traveled all around the city in a subway. I found out just how loud and fast a race car is. And I took a ferry boat to see the sparkling waves and the whistling sea gulls.

"I'm glad I found out about these things. But you know what, Kitty Cat? I didn't like waiting around for the storm to stop to fly the plane. I missed the bright blue sky when I was on the subway. The race car engines were too loud for me. And the boat made my stomach feel strange.

"I like driving my bus! I wonder what my new friends would think about my day? Maybe they're curious, too! I should send them each a letter inviting them to join me on my busy bus route," he said as he began searching for his pen.

Puzzles

Follow me!

Can you figure out where the plane, train, and bus are going? Follow the lines to see if you are correct!

airplane　　train　　bus

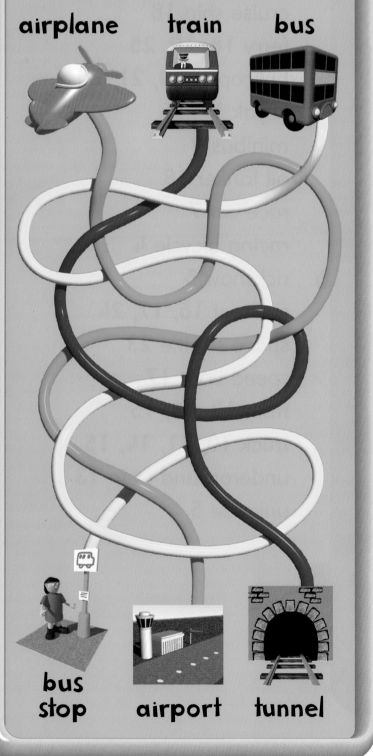

bus stop　　airport　　tunnel

Close up!

We've zoomed in on parts of things you have seen in this book. Can you figure out what you are looking at?

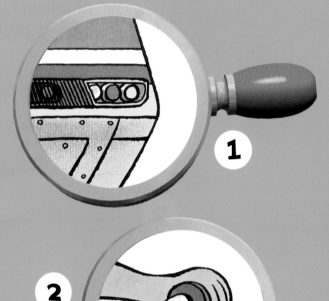

1

2

3

Answers: Close-up! 1 train locomotive and lights, 2 bicycle handlebar and bell, 3 ship smokestack.

EAU CLAIRE DISTRICT LIBRARY

EAU CLAIRE DISTRICT LIBRARY